PRAISE

Laurie Lynn Muirhead's evocative poems take the reader through the dual seasons of "winter and getting ready for winter" whilst living on a prairie ranch. From the Wolf Moon of January to the Strawberry Moon of June when the warmer weather "exfoliates sadness," both the physical and emotional landscape is beautifully and crisply wrought. These poems sing a powerful Coyote Snow song.

– Lynda Monahan, author of
A Slow Dance in the Flames, What My Body Knows, Verge,
and *The Door at the End of Everything*

Coyote Snow is a stirring love letter to season change, both physically and emotionally, on the sometimes stark, sometimes abundant prairie landscape. Muirhead uses her deft poetic hand to bring light to "gun-metal gray days," and pulls our attention "like the soft/purple face/of the crocus/skyward." This collection warms us, comfort us, and leaves us with lasting, hopeful images, like "lively yellow posies/in a coffee cup."

- Kim Mannix, author of *Confirm Humanity: Poems*

Coyote Snow is a prayer of love to the land in all it gives and takes, to its wild creatures, and to Muirhead's husband with whom she shares, "small dark whispers sweet as pulled taffy" and seeks shelter "when the wiles of life are just too much." With an abundance of grace, this collection explores what binds her to the land and the land to her, inviting the reader to reflect on their place in the vastness of this land which connects us all.

- Denise Wilkinson, author of the memoir
Like water to Breath

Laurie Lynn Muirhead's poems are a journey through the seasons which inspire me to retreat into the forest and live off the land. *Coyote Snow* is an exciting ode to nature which demonstrates spiritual alignment and mindful connection. If you are seeking presence and simplicity, these poems will remind you of the small details in life and their significance in the bigger picture. Captured within the poems are reminders of the power of the animal world and seasonal transitions in nature. Winter imagery, timely articulation, and honest contemplation successfully convey the challenging experience of life in the Canadian prairies.

- Drew Walker, author of *Confines of a Free Spirit* (2020) and *Closer to Closure* (2025)

Simple, the way a wild rose or the cry of a killdeer is simple. A sensual mix of the mystical and the precise. The business of living: scent of birth, touch of snow.

– Susan Musgrave, author of
Hunger: The Poetry of Susan Musgrave

POEMS

COYOTE SNOW

LAURIE LYNN MUIRHEAD

Wild Skies PRESS

Published 2025
Printed in Canada

ISBN Print 978-1-997770-01-5
ISBN Ebook 978-1-997770-02-2

Cover Design by Alexis Marie Chute
Cover Photo by Flo Dahm, Pexels
Interior Design by Alexis Marie Chute
Illustrations by Svetlana Soloveva, Aleksei Gur, and Saddako

For information address:
Wild Skies Press
A division of Alexis Marie Productions Inc.
Edmonton, Alberta, Canada
info@alexismariechute.com
www.WildSkiesPress.com

Wild Skies Press is an independent literary publisher founded in 2021. Wild Skies refers to the Aurora Borealis—northern lights—in Alberta, where the press is located, situated on Treaty 6 Territory. Wild Skies Press publishes non-fiction, fiction, poetry, and hybrid genres with an emphasis on the creation of Canadian works and books by emerging and established authors.
www.WildSkiesPress.com

*These poems are dedicated
to my brothers
Jerry, Bill, Terry
Rick & Mike
- and -
my father, Brony
(a bunch of land-lovers)*

COYOTE
SNOW

The first clean slate of snow,
a mapping of its residents,
the revelation of who goes where

CONTENTS

GETTING READY FOR WINTER

WINTER

WINTER

Be vigilant!
keep the fire in your brain
burning!

MELANCHOLY

Hello January
and how is the cold
dark side of you
the wanting warmth
of your not-too-tall days

Tell me
what light will you secrete
for the tepid thrum
of my existence
when I arise
in the dredge of your sleep
an oiled lantern
down the hall
flickering
          flickering
as hearts murmur
too brown toast with anhedonia

Is this really you?

your hefty fist of freeze
holding me implicitly
waiting and watching
the narrow vein of sunrise
imploding mercury?
          the slow pang
of melancholy mid-winter?

LOVE'S SLOW THAW

Winter
the calvary of white horse
gun-metal gray days
cast in the shadow
of almost no sun
her iron-clad words
lower than the sundogs
at high noon
slower than the coursing cold
running vertical
through horizontal vein
you and I working parallel
bundled abominably
exchanging orders
through thick balaclavas
your frosted eye fixed
on the frozen hose and flat tire
a twisted-up grin
when I scold you
for cursing this land
the seasonal existence
we so established

take discord to the shelter of a tepid barn
our seasonal displeasure with indifference
trouble-shoot the callous reality of your 40 below

with a composed kiss
on your cold cheek *love's   slow   thaw*
we embrace the brief respite of certainty
the warmest part of a man is a woman
                              her affections

LUNAR WOLF

Somewhere affection
perpetuates
      eternal warmth
      but not here
the consequence
of this northern post
forces the retreat
of a solar circumstance
the refraction
of more moon
      hiatus
      migration
      more sleep

Only the tenacious
endure the order
of the lunar wolf
pale breath heavy
with humidity
void of summer song
survival calculated
in the layers of fleece
shrouded by a roaring fire
in the milieu of a rich red wine

share with me the secret
of wood smoke and moon shine
the fire song of seclusion

BULLY BIRD

There is virtually
no song for January
the winter birds few in number
articulate cold and soft
an emulation of snow in keeping
with the balance of seasonal survival

But when I saw that chickadee
hanging from the beak
of the sparrow hawk
gaping wound   scourge of feathers

I was furious

that he would attack
my small winter song

furious

that he killed Chickadee
on my own front porch
her lifeless body
in the clutch of claws
her soft bit of trill   *silent*

And so
I meditated bird-murder
how I would set bait, a snare
pull sundogs into this war storm
make him feel dread and suffrage
something of his own affliction

but affliction in the natural world
halos the act of survival
and my anger is solely unjustified

FREEZE TAG

Unjustified?

this hoary hunger
of nocturnal foraging
in the dead of winter
wholly consumes
the ethereal twilight
of nonsensical anger

pale shadows slide
bare branches break
transcending weight
        of the wolf moon

I've attended
to the wolf moon
fire bright and hungry
the hard light
of her existence
searching   *more food*
how the mule deer
and the alpha bitch
bed in the spruce boughs
relentless ache
in the pit of their gut
who's stalking who
a chilling game of freeze tag
desperate transition
        surprise touch of death

FORBEARANCE

Just as the death-howl
of the loner wolf
cracks the white ache
      of winter
snowy owls seize the night
their icy wings
a ghost-ride
on the dark shadow
      of your forbearance
rebuking the cold moon's cry
      my heart words most certainly hide

consider
      the late winter sun mid-morning
      how it etches a new day within
      a warm cup of coffee
      the reconciliation of our quiet conversation

LOVESTRUCK

I remember the novelty
of our conversation
that slow cold February
my cupid coming of age
beside you in the cab
of your 79' Ford 4x4
starched pale blue jeans
paisley purple cowboy shirt
pressed warm against me

my soft vanilla musk
and sudden desire
deserted on the back road
void of anything but you
the quiet guy I watched
through strawberry shades
                of a teen crush

my anxious resistance
to becoming a woman
the barely woman you now held
in the quiet space
                of confession

your soft hand
in the cup of my chest
small dark whispers
sweet as pulled taffy

the snow falling hard around us
in the blue dark of all places
I should not be   *lovestruck*
                sensuous bits of fire
                into that cold dark night

SLOW SIMMER

These cold dark nights
     so obscure
     so hushed
a callous reception
of farm creatures subsiding
into a corralled rhythm
  of eat
     drink
     sleep
hibernation of wild-scape
and free-grazing on a slow simmer

And me
trapped in my own dormancy
cook and bake up a concerto
with the delicate scent of snow
pulling a low sun
into the dark corner of dining
brightened with blanched carrots
        green beans
        potatoes
a revival of the pot stew
some warm biscuits
your cow-conversation

three new births and a set of twins
in the cold, dead of night
it's your turn to sit with the moon

And the moon
holds vigil as I clean and refresh
the still white song of the snowy owl
the closing of sun-down and lunar-up
        Angel
        Nova and
        Lilah at the byre door
waiting for wheat straw and a warm bed
the primeval evolution of birthing your words
behind closed doors

VALENTINE'S DAY

There is praise for the seasonal
evolution
    amid
the estranged cupid
    of our existence

to the snap and crack
    of your dark mornings
breathing light
into my hot black coffee
into the burning end of short days

extending warm wool gloves
for my cool insipid hands
your thick wall of winter air
compressing empathy
for the living and the
    not-so-living
in this frigid state of survival

only the icy shatter
    of idle words
the decisive precision
    of your stockmanship
fracture the warming of a cold barn
these sharp bits on recoil
another premature birth with a dozen blue roses

and the intimate few words of forgiveness
    due morning

MESSENGER

Mourning the depth of snow
through the creek bottom to the cornfield
my every step a cold crescendo
in the dead quiet of bush branches
the sun, a shattering brilliance exfoliates sadness
      Bill is gone

It is mid-February and the cows are impatient
they line the horizon as soldiers calling out the order
for me to move the long stretch of wire so they can feed

Frozen chunks of tears litter my cheeks
      and I am ten again
Bill and I with our Christmas sleds
for tryouts on the paddock hills
his belly-laugh and red cheeks igniting the landscape
as we sleigh for hours despite the dark and the chill

A lone chickadee greets my weeping
at the turn of the bend
she sits quiet in the corn leaves only inches away
      me tucking
      Bill's memory into pockets with used tissue
      and the heaviness of the cold pliers
      to move the wire
She follows me like a little prayer
with soft chirps bouncing from leaf to leaf   *go away!*

The tears return as I walk the long length of corn
regret moving post to post, wire over wire
trying to ignore the bird, the absence of a
      goodbye
but the chickadee stays with me
flitting from stalk to stalk
her indulgent tone more excited
as we move further along
and I am abruptly annoyed that she won't allow sorrow
to hang with the sundogs
where my inner-self wants to be alone to mourn

As is the day, she is relentless,
her small bits of joy tango in the maize
infiltrating the gap of my brokenness
thru the softness of her elation, and suddenly
the wire sings with static and my hands are hot
as I strum the last length from post to post
and call-in the cows
the heralding vapour of the herd
somehow now a comfort
as their hooves and heads
crackle into the new space of corn
and they having feed,
I can finally be done with this field
with the excessive radiance of high noon,
make trudge for home

But the small bird flutters just ahead
beckoning me to a lone poplar tree
at the edge of the creek,
its every branch a shimmer of hoar frost
with a banditry of chickadees,
and my little messenger leaves me
to join their uplifting throng,
a resonation that Bill is at liberty
flying down heaven's home quarter hill
and I am so overwhelmed with this
                    Amazing Grace how sweet their song
the so suiting hymn he would have me sing
for the forgiveness of a winter burial

DARK WARRIOR

Forgiveness
perhaps the tolerance
of winter
embraces the gloom

the old moon indignant
bearing a grudge
his cold
    coppered face
reminiscent
of the dark warrior
unerring in his quest
for light
armoured with
the sword of Orion
he rehearses my plight
gallops into March
yielding the tranquil call
of a nearly spring night

come! oh long awaited spring
the birthing fields are ready to burst!

PAIN OF A WARM WOMB

The birthing fields
    are a seasonal ritual
    descent of root and seed
    dormant in a cold land
    resurrected with the pulling
    of the sun on longer days

Wide open spaces and soft gullies
speak fervent remembrance
bunches of poplar crowding
sunny-side of slough edges
and the lone call of a blue heron
extracts melody from warmer soil
and the old bones of something lost

Some days
cantankerous weather razes the land
she accepts her fate without dispute
pregnant cows abandon overt spaces
take shelter in willow brush and damp sod
labour gives no warning
              unpredictable
as the sudden chance of storm
birth falls where and when it will
           survival
strength of an abrupt delivery
        and a good mother

A good mother is of her own
        a spiritual psalm
she speaks to me when the sun pulls into itself
and the moon slides on the edge of coyote chorus
a hopeful chant that one might be stillborn
while the spicy scent of birth spills into the soil
            disappears

I know the pain of a warm womb

for it was I who ate the forbidden apple
                                not the cow
her contractions efficiently complacent
she licks placenta
swallows the afterbirth
sleeps on the edge   instinctive maternity

The birthing fields
are a daily dose of reverence
trusting the land
          this herd
          each other
fighting against the erosion
of what we know for sure
as if anything we say or do
will make a difference
for the night has long since concealed
any birthing calamities
                    some live
                    some die
and the coyote desires to eat too
          I grieve his rejoicing
          and the perceived notion
          that a good business
          should have no losses
          money is all that matters

but this is not about dollars and cents!
this is about humility
saving the weak, the premature, the rejected

for the delicate balance of any existence
          fragile

and our assistance with natural processes
        unwanted
An instinctual mama cow recedes
into the creases of the land
succumbs to labour and gives birth
on a virtuous day she claims victory
                renders an offspring

I only need to recognize,
how many virtuous days there are

DEATH IN A COLD LAND

There is nothing virtuous about a slow sun
depth of snow or belated equinox
the defiance of an east wind
                        her icy breath
                        traitorous heart
                        hurling blasphemy
                        frigid obscenities
                        into this already cold land

Holding this minute tepid body
a twin calf   birth abandoned
riding shotgun in the back of the quad
through a mirage of cold cattle and three weeks
of snow   wind   sleet   ice
                        a nerve-squall
nineteen hours since the last piece of toast
the last piece of good conversation
only a grievance of curses

this easterly witch just won't quit

And these words
                        seared with profanity
taunt the tempered cessation of this loquacious day
and perception can't see past this very second
                        and this very second
                        is all this calf might have
her rigid core wrapped in a wet blanket
clutching her like she was my first-born
in this belligerent wind
bone cold anguish
psychological distress
a simulation of the real war
                        unending atrocities
                        merciless slaughter
                        refugees for miles
                        anticipating rest
                        short on lung and breast-weary
babies too weak to suckle   fall prey

And I pray in a frenzied sort of anguish

hurry up!   she's not going to make it!

and the weight of this day
has brought the season's tribulation
      to a dark light
      and guilt for beseeching
      this one small calf
      finds morning
      suddenly selfish
when a world of hostility
abhorrent as this callous east wind
berates the land   rages on

And my rage is all but diffused
abruptly cold and hungry
balancing on the short side of defeat
I can only bestow what I know best
tube-feed and quilt wrap a cold calf
and tomorrow
      I shall make supplication
      stitch the fragility
      between breath and brawn
            sorrow and salvation
            life and death

Death in a cold land
      is death in a cold land
no closure of assurance
simple offering of peace
no finality of arrangement
with flowers
      a benediction
      or tea
just the shadowed cry of the raven
and the obliteration of what shall remain

UNTIMELY

The obliteration of winter
collapses into the ides of March
notorious for stormy weather
her seasonal assault sifts the land
from quarter to quarter
>   dead grasses bow
>   seared by grit
>   goggle-eyed calves
>   seek shelter within
>   their mother's udder

Another snow-birth
always untimely
small determined breaths
shifting
from bone to bone
all hope bent
no shelter
for all this stress
only a change of equinox
can dull this wind

and motivate the restitution of my veritable spring thaw

HEALING

Some days need a little restitution
when periodic snow buries the landscape
and the balance of birth and spiritual resilience
lay fraught beneath the encumbrance

I *know that to curse in times*
of nonsensical weather is of no use
what we live and experience on this land
excretes similar emotion regardless
of individual reaction and although we strive
for commonality   storm-stress ensues

And so
it was this day just after twilight
that I
with some reluctance
pulled on a pair of wool socks
                    wet mitts and
                    my parka full of farm
armed with a small torch
I trailed out into the indigo
a final check for snow-birth
and new mothers
and was wholly greeted
with an erotic pink moon
in a sky full of bird lullaby

It was a warm dark hug of cool spring air
squeezing time and tension into a sweet salve
                    for all the raw edges

It was the slough song of a goose and a gander
the gentle heart-pull of a robin's return
                    bidding me

rest, all is well   we will choir-up for what is lost

It was absolutely not what I was expecting
                    healing

SANCTUARY

On occasion
winter's demise
denies me
the raw fringe
of an emotive
      healing
allowing
the strain of today
to spill over
tomorrow's shoulders
the frugality of knowing
when and how to concede

And so
I rally the worm moon
her earthy utterance
from the floor
of the boreal forest
spicy pine
cinnamon willow
organic poplar
zesty chokecherry
and sugary maple
arouse appeasement
revitalize persona
elevate the very essence
of intention
her leaves
      bark and
      limbs
a sanctuary for my cold bones

HARKEN

Mornings
so much brighter now
the fresh lungs of April
prepare a sanctuary
for the riotous sun
as she craves absolution
petitioning the snowfall
             to cease

her reclamation
of the crow's nest
is most certain
flocks congregate
their conversant chatter
amid the ides
harken the awakening
a change in my weather

BREAK-OUT SMILE

Is that you spring?
tossing your stiff
leather rigging
worn chaps
sunny-side up
an April-shower
of wild wind
breaking free
from a callous winter
of snow-deep days
and a face full of fur

Time to shave
the mean memoir
of frostbite
and dark, dark, dark
emerge
from the glacier
of a raw season
pallid skin aching
for the delicate touch
of a woman's fingers
and the warmth
of an amorous chinook

These cold days
you will sever and toss
your break-out smile
always holding back
the new growth
of a winter's tide
the distant horizon
of snowy memories

I wait for the migratory birds
the certainty of spring on the wings of striving

SPRING BREAK

This day is for the birds
the sage grouse
the black-billed cuckoo
for the snow goose
her migratory flight
sun-struck and starry-eyed
she follows a pink moon
making spring break
    on the eve
of the hummingbird season

Her willowed breath
tightly woven
in the delicate threads
of a wren's nest
linger in the heart strings
of a song sparrow
while the early morning mist
    aloof
in the meadow's muted drum
sends a ghostly pleasure
of killdeer to bluff
any invasion of tranquility

Only the warbler disputes
    her peace
is with the mourning dove
and a tufted titmouse
a quarrel of forgiveness
    bird praises
sure, as the prayer of flight

A MEMORY'S REMINDER

It was this day
in the soft willow of prayer
that I sat in the Utley grazing paddock
a high point where I could watch
        for the coyote
        his broken ambling
        gut-hungry jaunt
the wayward freedom
of his existence
the mindful question

who is the trespasser?
him or I?

Despite his elusive presence
the aroused aura of near dusk
abruptly collided with his uncanny chorus
        and the alarmist lament
of a killdeer's cry at the dugout's edge

I held breathless
the scent of birth-leaf
and pussy willow
the emergent silence of crested wheat
          and reed canary
a memory's reminder

you are an emulation of the good shepherd
when feeding and checking
when birthing and treating
when guarding the herd
beyond any ill-fated sentiment

And just now, for this one time
I need the coyote to be full of rabbit and passing by

KILLDEER HEART

What is it about the passing of coyote snow
the sumptuous essence of thaw

Is it the soft scent of bloom
   chokecherry
   wild rose
   ornamental crab?

Is it the devout remembrance
   of green buds
   and pussy willow
   the long song of sun
   zealous with new birth
   and prenatal slough water?

Is it the amphibious recall
of wanting
my green rubber boots
        polka-dot umbrella
        father's steeped tea
        mother's fresh buns
        the old red barn with the calico kittens?

Or is it my very first kiss
        in the buttercup meadow
        and the strawberry moon
        of our quiet beginnings
        in the hurried cry of your killdeer heart?

it's the resurrection of your warm words
after a cold winter

RESURRECTION

A craft of kites
flutter the gust
of a spring squall
pulling the soft
purple face
of the crocus
skyward

a resurrection
of warmth
and jubilation
the dandelion
instigating
the small hand
of forgiveness   rejoices!

lively yellow posies
in a coffee cup on my dinner table

GETTING READY FOR WINTER

*Winter is over for the lay of the land
but never for the steward of the mind*

WOMEN AND THE LAND

Finally
light and warmth
the darkest of days
all but a memory
soft spring rain
and new growth
washing over
the snow scars
of an overly
ambitious winter

Time to dream a garden
plant some poesy
let the blooms breathe in

And so
I measure and mark
pound stakes
spray wire-weed
work fingers
and loam to death
and naturally
the song of soil
with the long arm
of an old sun
heartens me to crawl
out of my cold skin

Where to begin?
perhaps
a shrub-garden
with popsicle lilacs
dazzling daylilies
maybe some
patio stones, red
and rustic
burnished browns
toppled with

wooden whiskey barrels
begonia-jammed
and spilling over
the kind you could
get drunk on
lazing in a braided hammock
sipping the evening air

Or perhaps
some vegetables
whisper of carrot seed
and leaf lettuce
along side rows and rows
of sunflowers
   squash and
   kohlrabi
the spiritual poise
of heat and humidity
pulsating the seed
pouring from the sun
                into soil
                into me

what is it about women and the land?

wombs for the seed
nurturing the roots
their gardens
so much more
than fresh fruit
and vegetables
bouquets or borsch
a whole pot of healing

life begins when you plant a garden
                Chinese Proverb

PAPER MOON

genuine life begins when you have children
a never-letting-go of apprehension

On de-junking the spare room
a paper moon arose from the horizon
of old report cards and childhood crafts
for mom and dad   scribbled on the back

And I think of all your moons
                    I have survived
each one wholly anticipated
falling break-neck into the earth
resurrected with the orbital pull
of moving me forward
                    around and around

How so many times wanted to pull
your fire from the sky
conquer the hot season of your nearly
                    summer solstice

But there was no chance exploiting
                    any such conflagration
when you burned late into the nerve of puberty
I lay with the moon anxious with not knowing
                    where are you?
some bush party
dancing up a bonfire
                    with life
                    infatuation
                    intoxicating barley spirits

full moon   full moon   full moon

Could only guess your destination
hoping you'd find the short path home
spare the weight of my worry
in bed before midnight

a misfire of hope

blue moon   blue moon   blue moon

It was the psalmist who assured me

your children are a heritage, speak wisdom
and they shall return with an open bone of perception

Today we share the moon in the same light
                  a bonfire
                  with marshmallows
                  hot chocolate
celebrate the mystery
of the cosmic evolution
your coming of adulthood
                  a total eclipse

And now
I hold this chipper moon
the simple weight of paper and all your fire
                  triumphant!

ELATION

Triumphant monarchs
make
seasonal flight
arrive
with the torch
for summer solstice
ornamented
yellow
orange
and white
they precipitate elation

tranquillity   and long hours of labouring light

BLUE DIAMOND
(FOR BEV)

One tranquil day on this land
is as rare as the blue diamond
coyote wary and
        spiritually unassailable
I was procreated
      to make hay
      feed stock
      ride miles of tough grass
my saddle sores and sick calves
      surely amended

Weather-wise
I play the clouds with a braided rope
pull petition into each coil
flanking my partner
      on the prairie
      in the barn
      at the bank
know the prudent side of a hard dollar
what to do with a profit and
when there is not

My persistence breaks trail
and after hours are nothing new
with a casserole in the oven
and a baby at my breast
I repair old denim
      worn socks
the unsung melody of no regret

And only
when all things are fed
        safe
        in place

do I crawl into slumber
my wind-burnt skin laced with lavender
                        warm flannelette
a silhouette of salt and prayer
I sleep on the short side of tomorrow

FOSTERING

On the short side of ritual
the longest day
of a late spring gathering
snatches me up
in the yearly cavalcade
of horses and hats
tack and trailers
an assembly of rough stock
and tough hands
ready to ride the buck off the sun
for a few beers
and the reciprocal trade
of instinctual knowledge
that comes with living the land
                tending livestock

Their round-up
slow and methodical
easy on horse and herd
allows the lullaby of the land
                to hold true
the cow-calf connection
a mentality of trusting
rider-horse positioning
and the stockman's golden rule

treat your neighbor's cows
as you would have them treat yours
...

Bestowed with the promise
of unwritten liability
stockmen arrive unexpectedly
and stay till the job is done
or the moon quietly shuts them down
when the bone-talk and
          beer-jargon
          between meat and potatoes

speaks furtively on the whispering
                of a good horse
how a few oats
and a little sugar talk
pulls the gentle eye
and soft mouth
of any worthy steed
an alliance of conviction
and cow-sense
even the raunchiest brute won't outsmart
...

Somewhere between sun-up and
                    sun-down
a sage stockman exists
shepherding the earthly timeline
of his borders
a fostering of calf and coyote
                native grass
                willow bluff
                how to read a warning sky
                and the dog's sudden deviation

He values the unwritten salt of his worth
where he came from and ultimately
            where he will end up
and he knows at the closing of each day
how to make supplication
                for all things he could not mend

SUMMER SOLSTICE

Supplication
on this
the brightest day
of the year
rallies the cosmic
blue aurora
to stand
momentarily
hushed
a resounding
exhortation
for the reality
of longer days
the ritual sowing of sustenance

And ever should I weaken
burn a small hole of doubt
into the hands of my aging
I'll catch myself breathless
        fencing
        new lands
        over-ambitious
        paddocks
        at the sacrificial
        burning-out
        of my summer solstice

dance with me the long song of sun
when old love and light entangle
        for this one jubilant day

ENRAPTURED

Jubilant days
  of amiable sun
and rain showers
  utilize
the unending
  length
of infinite light
  naturally creating
a melody
  of morning dew
enraptured
  in my thriving
of all things incarnate

we've endured hundreds of seasons in sync
with the land and the livestock
      the cold and the dark
      new life and regrettably, death

our colours now changing
from summer blonde to winter white
      dimples to wrinkles
      our holding hands to holding on
there is something different about this kind of love

EARTH AROMA

There is something
about sun-peek
at 3:00 AM, when
the warbling arousal
of bird-song explores
the not-so-sound
of my sleep
and suddenly
I am overly awake
ready to quick-coffee
hit the hayfield

Raking hay
when dewdrops
are feverish
in a mosquito buzz
is all its own
a farmgirl's gift
the earth-aroma
of curing alfalfa
something
that can only
be sensualized
in the damp moments
between rake and roll

Wearing sheer
determination
rubber boots
and a straw hat
I fire up the Fordson
grease the rake tines
search the horizon
for a lavender sky
my inherent proverb

rise early, work hard
and make hay while the sun shines

WHOSE STORM?

Whose perceived endurance?
with the shine of a dull sun
the abrupt whirling, unfurling
of your sudden rain-squall
my upholding of clemency
               always
for the miracle of calm

Whose storm?
when all hell is bent
on uprooting the field
            my begonias
            the loosen shingle
            leaning shed
            the old red barn
            my one last nerve
...

Should have anticipated
storm on the radar
a week of high humidity
            exhaustive heat
taunted by thunder-fight
hurled hail stones
pitched a plow wind
         uprooted spruce
         and poplars
         the robin's nest
blue ragged shells empty
         and gaping
embryos lost to the sun

Despite fate   she warbles
a perfect psalm of sorrow
compromising her demise
spurs me into action
picking broken limbs
making sacrificial piles
I forge ahead in the spirit of a robin's remorse

SHATTERED

There is
a remorseful beauty
in the soft edge
of storm
the pale white
of cumulus
taunting
her cynical grays
a black boiling point
steering
for no direct hit
non-determined
by wrath or quilt or sin

She arrives
without warning
air pressure pouting
cold then hot
kicking up the dust
lurching
end over end over end
a barn-burner
of a disaster
casting her cold
crystal tears
into the hands
of my come-of-age garden   shattered

*I make supplication under the quiet light of the moon
for the healing of bruised pumpkins, the redemption of
brokenness*

MIDNIGHT INTERCESSION

Some nights
are full of redemption
when I ignore the moon
expounding
the urgency for sleep
her quiet psalm of slumber
tucked secretly beneath
the maze of starlight
         starbright
           first star I seek
is usually midnight

for midnights
are more than
      reservation
more than
      a few small wishes
scattered amid
moon-stream and
slough shadows

it's the slow damp air
pressing the stress
from my farmer's lung
like a slice
of warm lemon pie
and a weak cup of tea
it's the sweet taste
of the after-dark
the midnight's intercession

the cool breath of late evening
revitalizes a wearied persona
prepares me for the next long day

AMENS

Just as the long days
necessitate the pull
of soil and sun
dusky bonfires
spark hotdogs
  marshmallows
  royal red wine

the August trail of livestock
was not without mishap, fifteen
missing, mommas and babies
the search through heavy brush and
searing heat too many hours
wearied the horses, tempered
our morale, early dusk
settling the score you're done!

we unsaddle under the soft light
of a quarter moon. the shadowy
taste of heavy dew summoning shivers
and the horses restless with mosquitos
and hunger cooperate, they want
their home paddock and so do I

this ritual for the shepherdess
seeking solace
  when
the gathering of birds
and the loner coyote
make a festive communion
  for all her amens

tomorrow is a new dilemma
and we will return with fresh mounts
renewed hope and no strategy

AMOROUS PSALM

It was never a dilemma
when late nights
were a small space
of communing
and the pull of a long day
held no victory
in the shadows
of a slow moon rising
for puerile blood
held its own heat
long after the sun retired
on hot motors and
    sore muscles
when hoisting bales and
        pounding nails
left no trace
of a cursed sweat
consumed in the serenity
of a love-affair
long anticipated
in the short moments
between brain and brawn

It was great to be young
when working the land
spilled over
        into holding
        the land-lover
the rigidity
of the day's labour
dismissed amid
the rise and fall
of the night owl's
amorous psalm
the relentless August heat
of unseasoned affection   instinctual desire

our slumber breathes the sweet scent of summer
holds us momentarily in the small space of tenderness

WHAT DOES IT MATTER
(in memory of the Wild Rose drought, 2002-2003)

The summer fields have suffered
no moisture for weeks
cursed with heat
their tender faces
sustain nothing
no forage
      grasshopper
            or gopher
all has abandoned this dry-grass season
...

So desperately dry
each day we pray and water
my garden
your sunflowers
pots of petunias and peonies

You ask
why doesn't God harvest his pumpkins
so, we can listen to them thunder into his cellar

My voice is dry as scorched earth
beneath our feet
words all but withered   *all we can do is wait*
...

It's been three months   *still no rain*
the barley field long past suffering
                 is dead
and the buck moon
his dry freeze inevitable
plays lethal on the cold side of calamity
only a warm rain can restore your smile
...

After the winter the soil is desiccated
not much snow leaves me wondering

what will happen this season?
will it rain or not   *should we plant or wait?*

The snow geese return
dry slough beds cracked
            bleed instinct
water or no water
they sow their seed in faith

I tell you   *so should we*
plant wheat
        barley
        and conviction
into the dry earth   *will new life grow?*
even our assurance lies dormant
...

Thought last year was tough
just four inches of rain
barely enough feed
minimal straw
sold down the cows
culled hard
  poor udders
    cracked feet
      ugly attitudes
refinanced our plans

Now
things are much worse
only one inch of rain
            no feed
            no straw
            no plans
...

I hold this land
in the spiritual script
of my own rejection

willow bluffs shelter
for a melancholy soul
she's been here forever
rooted me deep in sandy soil
her face fresh with spring rain

Two years of drought
have left her with dry breasts
            a miscarrying womb
like her   *thirsty for rain*
            your smile
            slake conversation
this holding back because of drought
you never held back before
            but then
there's never been a drought
            and you
not knowing what to do
have wilted like the wheat field
            and I know too well
if this dryness doesn't end
no amount of rain will save us
...

Heard your voice at midnight
warned me of the winter
summer kitchen cold as ice
the frost between the bed sheets

Tear down the fence between us
burn it with all bitterness
smoldering embers of love once lost

Really   *what have we lost?*
the fire's been gone
            for weeks
            months
and we're still together
an obligation

full of empty words
        empty grain bins
        empty dugouts

what does it matter?
a field without water   our lives without love

TERRACOTTA SEASON

Does it matter
that I was born in the cold?

called from the matrix
of my mother's womb
my face set like flint
walking in the light of her fire
in the sparks she kindled
as a root out of dry ground

my longing was always
the warmth of her summer garden
soft loam and a desirous sun
the respiration of the earth
              and the leaves
an emotional migration
with that of the hummingbirds
their honeyed-affection
stretching prayer-fold
as the Pale Beauty
into the vulnerability
of a new moon
and the tepid fingers
of this terracotta season
my warm August palate
              always
refusing to shed her seasonal skin

it matters that my first breath was that of winter
bronchitis, croupe, a cold baby survivor
the snow-scape rejoicing, code-blue

THE IRONY OF TUMBLEWEED

Was it you that survived the cold
the piney rosin of leathered seasons
  prairie wool
  and pigweed
  wrestling the land
through those hard stony years
dirty thirties of grasshoppers
and century deep snow
putting your profit to death
not to mention the spring squalls
     of wind and more wind
    blowing soil and sanity
      ditch-side
the irony of tumbleweed?

But then, it was you who said
  what makes a man can't break him
as you recall standing adjacent to the tail gales
witching water with a willow
making pickets from crooked poplar
and stitching the same leather boots
    sole on soul
a penny saved is a penny earned
    nothing less

And now
you reminisce of loving the land and a woman
in the same breath
  your progeny wired to carry on
allowing you to become the lemonade stand
  on the front porch
  selling your wisdom
  in the sour flavor of urgency
before the earth comes calling for your bones

ESSENTIALITY

The bones of early autumn
for the sake of sound reason
render lukewarm offerings
the not quite harassment
    of white-laced breath
    and icy camouflage

I ignore the thought
allow lemonade to revel
in the low heat
of a waning equinox
her soft pale yellow
    liquid sour
warm as cold could ever be

Yet cold
covets the moment
demands the spotlight
    ice cubes in black tea
    ice water for dehydration
shaved ice in snow cones

she will not let me forget
her essentiality for all seasons

there is something beneficial with essentiality
like being wrapped in the wings of the wind
the discreet persistence of Seraphim

CLUTCH OF MEMORY

There is nothing beneficial
with the seasonal mourning
of coloured leaves
and the waning call
of the snow goose
when the first breath of frost
makes cornstalks wilt
and nasturtiums weep
a fluent reminder
bone-chill and ice-talkers

The earth's wisdom
is with all creatures
instinctually wired
the squirrel's ability
to store summer
in a clutch of memory
of scarlet roses and
soft-scented honeysuckle
alive with hummingbirds
who flit and fiddle
a chaos of color
high speed bee-bombers
splitting the sound barrier
of a straw-hat day

So vital
these bits of remembrance
as the oil for my stove
and the bread in the oven
I'll feast on this stash
of warm memories
when the mercury hits thirty below

the sudden fire-storm of forest leaves
and the elusive shift of sunlight
a calculated alarm not to be ignored

FALSE HEAT

Mid-September and time to calculate
the fruitions of an earthly womb
a ritual of readiness
when the soil grows weary
and mellow seeds will soon lay dormant
                              in cold caskets

But not today
summer lingering in the laziness
of an unexpected burst of heat
her sultry palate hanging on the fruits
of a pregnant garden
fourth trimester   full and overripe
            pulls at my guilty bones
            three laundry baskets of peas
            forty quarts of dill pickles
            blanching beans with the milky way

Too much I say   rally the sisters
a seasonal gathering of sundry hands
for winter harbours a spirit of non-giving
her cold shoulder teasing the uncertainty
                      of a false heat
an urgency of preservation within gallons
                  of red romas and juicy gossip
                  seasoned with jalapeños
                  those cantankerous hot peppers
                  and a crash of celery

This sizzling salsa brewed in the heat
of a spoiling of words
our fiery tongues sacrificed
                  double portioned
                  with refiner's salt
                  a cleansing of pure vinegar
                  the pressure cooker on a holy high

LEAN

The high prairies
can be voracious
vast stretch of needle grass
and blue sky consume us
on any given day
so much a part
of this wild-scape
in love with the land and a good horse
we saddle-pack minutes
                  into hours
                  into days
                  and months
herding a system of values
not many know a darn thing about

Our drove
of strong breeding and do-ability
left to the lean flank of skint soil
bring home a profit
and winter flesh on their bones

Lean is all we know
                  meagre meals
                  poor pay
                  and the wind
                  hard from the west
plays insanity with the far borders
                  of a weak mind

A leaning tree
on the lone savannah
doesn't know
the straight side of tomorrow
                  and us
crooked caballeros at sundown
lean into the heat of the land
sleep the saddle-side of a sore moon

URGENCY

The moon's premonition
of an imminent frost
    charges
enamored hummingbirds
to feed more often

tolerant of all things
envisioned
the robin discerns
also, the urgency
    of migration

how the sun pulls
her further south
beyond the far side
    of ever-darkening

the subtle exposure
    of cooler nights
and the pressing veracity
    of having to calculate
the processing of field corn into silage

I sleep with the autumnal moon
a blushing ball of hesperidium
cautioning: winter's just ahead

WINTER ANGST

The moon more often now
with shallow light
fervent repose
you in a stupor of silence
   sour cream and
   sauerkraut
   sour milk dripping
the cream separator
   sticky dry
flies buzzing backlash
their gauzy wings immobilized
membranes cracked
harvester defunct
and so, you slump
into the long shadow of autumn
your bowl full of winter angst

rice pudding?
would you like a cup of tea?

you mumble
shake your head
and without a glance
abandon the table
   the teapot
   my sink
   full of dirty dishes
the weight of ironstone
and Corningware
steel wool cutting away
   another supper
with no salt and quiet politics

how easy to buy newness for what is broken
but salt in an old wound embitters
unpretentious forgiveness is only of a supple heart!

ONLY TWO SEASONS

And so, as expected
the reserved empathy
of a solar dispute
embitters the edges
of a false heat
her mirage of sun dogs
racing urgency
of snowstorm
after a warm Thanksgiving Day
when the moon agreeably slides
        behind cold clouds
        obliging the wild goose
        to swell above the assault
of a snowy barrage
waist-deep drifts
my legacy of survival
        and the abrupt reality

on this land there is the quiet deception
of only two seasons
winter, and getting ready for winter

FROSTBITE

The ides of October
astute with the chill
of an intimate deception
chase burnished leaves
that razzle-dazzle
find refuge in the song
of the painted ponies
their cool caramel nights

Trick or treat   defeat
the buck moon quarrels
on the edge of autumn
with dog-faced bats
who hover and squawk
a terror of hoarfrost

My summer spirit spooked
refuses dormancy
feasts on a solstice
of stored sunshine
balmy midnights with bonfires
scorched marshmallows
old-time coffee
from a tomato can
something warm
for a genuine frostbite

soon after, the white language of winter
will meditate her early return

SEARCHING

When snow comes early
the soil claims a new language
her tired talk of a cold
                    suppression
urging earthworms
to crawl eight feet to the frost line
                    migration?
                    hibernation?
it's a worm thing and they are warm

But above ground
squirrels hurry to check
their storage hutches
full of nuts and seeds
for thieves such as field mice
                    and magpies
                    who chatter
                    and scatter
when the sparrow hawk
zones in on his own feast
and the snow now crimson
with scattered feathers
leaves nothing for the imagination
of the red fox in search of free food

My home town
            main street
            gracious souls
            serving coffee
            and muffins
to those like the red fox
searching for their next meal
            a warm space
            and perhaps   one meagre smile

the harvest, abundant or not
obliges that of a genuine thanksgiving
the bequeathing of all things blessed

MIDNIGHT MARCH

An over abundance
of harvested wheat
and bearded barley
converge
within steel bins
yielding something
of a blessing
for weary hands
and the ingathering
of light from the hallowed moon
her ashen face peppered
with wayward geese
     flouting
the midnight march
of small people
        pumpkins
        ghosts and
        goblins
intending
to raid the good side
of my candy-coated disposition

SNOW ON THE GROUND

Something about this day
my reserved disposition
when the low spark of November
strangely surrenders no snow
                              no ice
the geese
with their long slender necks
haggling in the slough
seemingly non-observant
to the finality of autumn
the pull of pathways only they perceive

And so, I scrutinize them
water-diving, preening
sunning themselves
on the shores of short days
and think perhaps I too
can sip a slow read on the sun porch
the last few pages of
A Clear Summer's Night
oblivious to the waning equinox
the precise deception
of a much-lamented clipper

But oh, I am so much wiser now
been fully caught with my Stanfield
underwear down and my toes
frozen in rubber boots
cattle storm-stayed miles from home
furnace filter dirty, carrots in the ground
and the gutters full of leaves

And I know, just as my wishes
scatter amid the galaxy
of cold stars and migratory song

the geese will surely take flight at midnight
leave me the vacancy of slough water
    and thin ice
    their soft downy dreams
      snow on the ground

COMMEMORATION

I have almost come to terms
with embracing
the first clench of snow
when the subtle glow
of harvest lanterns
are just a flicker
on the far edge of the western sky
and the land now cooling
her stubbled face
             dormant
allows me to let go of my longer days

There is something to cherish
with the loss of leaves
the nakedness of deciduous trees
a commemoration of sacrifice
                 soil
                 seed and
                 soldier

you and I can breathe at length now
the restitution of gentler days, unhurried words
kindle for a slow burning fire

GOOD FORTUNE

How do you breathe bear
in your snug den
curled round and snail-like
or perhaps long and languid

Do you settle deep into autumn
the cold swirling
madly about your door
            whispering   *sleep bear sleep*
for the high bush cranberry
is portioned for the grouse
and the field of oats
have been stolen for the bin

There is nothing left for you
except the gift of good fortune
and five months of sleep
while the rest of us keep
            the slow dark days
            of your birch bark flaming
            the long white hunger
            for your summer sun

my life has become that of coyote snow
the intricacy of all my trials and trails
more visible with the first abrupt layer of winter

COYOTE SNOW

On searching
the November paddocks
remnants of yearly losses
arouse anxiety
polished bones
sinew-less and scattered
conceal a bitterness
with the first skiff of coyote snow

And all about me
is a deathly quiet
the land holding sacred
a camouflage of secrets
now revealed in mounds
of fresh dirt polka-dotting
the snow-scape   thought provoking

what happens below the frost line?

the slow breath
of the small brown rodent
sedated sleep in a dug-out den
or perhaps a shallow grave?

These mounds
spewed from desperate claws
the badger knows hibernation all to well
he feasts on low flesh   *lowly gopher*
    a surprise attack
    total annihilation
    a war zone without boundaries
generals in the food chain doing what nature intended

IMMINENT

The intentions
of late autumn
arise from the earth
shifting with the high
and low of the land

the musky scent
of expiration
heeds me to a cold
remembrance
the foreseeable
mantle of white
sealing the season
down under
where moles and
brown bears sleep
their slow breath
a small tremble
in my apprehension
the notion
that we should be on over-ride
searching the gullies
        swamps and
        pine bushes
where stray cattle wild as they may be
        won't outsmart us
        and I in the kitchen
        cooking the midnight brew
will keep a vigilance of ready words
        to prop you up
        on the fourteenth hour
when the assault of winter is all but imminent

WITHOUT CAMOUFLAGE

The assault
of an early winter
laments in the nakedness
of tree branches
without camouflage
I see more vividly
the certainty of death
for some small creatures

A lone coyote
lingers too close
I watch him scrounging
for something   *anything*
his mangy body
idling down with the mercury
cold is not kind
to a fellow with very little fur

I want to gift him warmth
in some way, but I know
this is not my business
tomorrow's forecast
will surely look after him
a small quiet bump
under the fresh quilt of snow

WINTER

In the heart of winter
one can always find within themselves
small bits of summer!

WINTER SPICE

There is a solace
in the soft scent of snow
the sudden wake
of baring branches
winter spice
a momentary amendment

There is a longing
in the proclamation
of the night owl
frozen pond shivers
her spiritual script
blistered in a low sun

There is wanting
on the visionary side
of the moon
the lunar halo calls out
for my losses
obscures my seasonal wounds

there is a solace this day, if only for me
renewal in the promise of a low sun

PERMISSION

And so as was tradition
the ritual promise that we
would set out at high noon
in canvas coats and mended coveralls
with a hacksaw and an axe
to the far end of the river paddock
a great spread of forest
against the sliding sundogs
of a mid-December day
the low winter sun holding vigil
                              against expectancy
as we trudged into the canopy of green
the discreet revelation of deer beds
                              squirrel hutches
                  and the great blue spruce
that would ultimately grace
the corner of our small festive kitchen

Directing me back you swung hard
the cold crack a grimace
the small ache of echo
sawing yourself tired
as we trimmed and pulled
the massive bush
through hefty terrain
            knee-deep snow
the last few feet a push of expectation
as if now the lacerated trunk not quite fresh
could see the anticipation of bright lights and tinsel
            your sudden declaration

I left a good height of trunk
and should we return summer-side
there will be new growth and permission to cut again

a tree heavily pruned offers new growth
and the quiet wisdom from the forest floor
produces an over abundance of seasonal mercy

BEMOANING

This day
seemingly merciless
the winter tempest
          besieged
the first hour
of the moonless solstice
a ring around
the sun for days
warned me
of the coming
wind-whipping
the layers of drift
waist-deep
even hibernation
would be left winded
and the sparrow
without shelter
found her way
into the certainty
of a white grave
her sudden stillness
          a ransom
for no slumber
       crush of ice water
       tired limbs
song of the woodland dog
       bemoaning

I seek shelter in you, my friend and paramour
when the wiles of life are just too much

THE SACRIFICE

Like an old friend
the aroma of raw pine and sugar-spice cookies
revisit the memory of a shared season
the slower days of dark fruitcake
and death by Pot Of Gold chocolate
when small Chinese mandarins were a rare treasure
found in the bottom of a grey woollen sock
alongside hard ribbon candy and a new toothbrush

Like an old song
the melody of winter wind
and the crack of a cold house
played its own festive instrumental
with the cookstove at midnight
roaring with the hot tune of tamarack
and the quiet heat of our side-by-side
became evidently crucial
at the eye-wink of morning
when the wood smoke and fire song
were all but a wisp in a pile of cold ash

Like an aged wine
the taste of communion
with exaltations and candlelight
retold in the story of shepherds in teacloth
and Mary with her dolly
small kings of humility and tinseled angels
prepared our hearts for a pensive reflection
of the gift and the sacrifice
our love for one another
if only united for this one blessed night

conviction is the sharing of sacrifice in all seasons
a constant reminder of the sincerity of a warm heart
to not let the cold slip between
the palette of faith and survival
the untamed reality of our winter song

WINTER SONG

The summer trill in my heart
knows the way of the snowy owl
how she sleeps with her feathered face
    closed
to the circle of the sun
    closed to the brilliance
of snow-dreams mid-morning
how her iciness holds me
in the quiet space of confession
    ever mindful
of what needs to be done
and *who! who! who!* should do it

The summer trill is quiet now
unable to speak of
what the winter solstice
has always known
how the sun
      moon
      and stars
are spiritually positioned
anchored to the grid of locale
and if I wanted eternal warmth
    I should not be here
in this catch-all of seasons
    I should not be here
with the snowy owl
her nocturnal language
the quiet testimony of her winter song

FREE FALLING

In the beauties of holiness
from the womb of the morning
the dew of a brother's testimony
                    lay dormant
in the lullaby of a late autumn
                    lamentation
            the layering of
            warm sacred leaves
            confessing their expiration
            in the sage of his not-surviving
            another old-man winter

and suddenly
not so beautiful
but wonderful

the wisdom of knowing
that death can only take the body
a remembrance void of
skin, scars, and bone
the spirit of his laughter
      free
            falling
into the glory of all things made new

> *"in the beauties of holiness*
> *from the womb of the morning"*
> *Psalm 110:3*

LOVE-LANGUAGE

The coyote is calling in the new year
a glorious song of not-hungry
      he is happy this night
his words catch me-up at near dusk
when the sun is so low, I can almost taste
the warmth of her belly and the snow
now blushing with sunset harmonizes
the delight of his estranged chorus

She howls back, a distinct smooth cackle
the cold carrying her sweet-scented notes
on the frozen tips of tree branches
the hoarfrost falling between the membranes
of her highs and lows the soft-aching crescendo
of surprise
      ahh   the coyotes are courting

Ensnared in their vibrato
the silkiness of shiver dances
aurora borealis, a collision
of desirous song and consuming colour
synchronizing the love-language
of the heavens and the unknown certainty
      how am I a part of this

Regrettably

the time-loss of sharing gathers me unaware
that it is snowing now and I am cold
the coyotes are quiet and the colour is gone
my porch light, a small beacon of welcome
appeals to me
and I leave the secrets of this night where they belong
tomorrow I am assured
      there will be two sets of tracks
      in the coyote snow

*"How many lessons of faith and beauty we should lose,
if there were no winter in our year!"*

Thomas Wentworth Higginson

ACKNOWLEDGEMENTS

Thank you to my family for their love, patience, and encouragement over my many hours spent with pen and paper. And to the members of *sans nom poetry group*, each and every one of you, for being the first audience for most of these poems. Your critique and editing helped shape many of these poems into what they are today.

I would like to recognize the Saskatchewan Writers' Guild for all their professionalism when it comes to the writing community. They make accessing information and support regarding all aspects of writing attainable.

And finally, with special gratitude, a big thank-you to Alexis Marie Chute and her team at Wild Skies Press for seeing the worth in this manuscript. Their guidance, attention to detail and expertise is second to none. It's been an absolute privilege to work with this publishing house!

NOTES

Earlier versions of these poems have appeared in the following publications:

"Winter song" – Lilac Arch Press
"Blue Diamond & Lean" – Saddlebag Dispatches
"Paper Moon" – The Society
"Spring Break" – Canadian Contemporary Poetry Anthology
"What Does it Matter" – CBC Radio

ABOUT THE AUTHOR

Laurie Lynn Muirhead is the author of two previous books: *Bone Sense* (poetry) published by Thistledown Press and *Lullaby Lilly* (children's picture book) published with Your Nickel's Worth Press. She is a long-standing member of *sans nom poetry group* and a current member of the Saskatchewan Writers' Guild.

Laurie Lynn has spent thirty-five years employed with the Saskatchewan Rivers School Division, first in special education, and currently as a librarian. Through creative writing workshops and in-school poetry programs presented over the past twenty-five years, she has mentored youth from kindergarten through Grade 12. She lives in beautiful North Central Saskatchewan with her husband, Ward, in the rural area of Wild Rose. She has two sons, Justin and Casey, two lovely daughters-in-law, Amanda and Hally, and grandchildren, Stran, Sawyer, Flint & Hutch. When she is not writing, Laurie is helping out on the family ranch, gardening, and rooting for the underdog.

Other Books from Wild Skies Press

www.WildSkiesPress.com

www.ingramcontent.com/pod-product-compliance
Lightning Source LLC
Chambersburg PA
CBHW071209120626
46546CB00006B/2482